LEVEL
2

Planets

Elizabeth Carney

NATIONAL
GEOGRAPHIC

Washington, D.C.

For Professor Xavier Creary
—E. C.

Special thanks to Marianne J. Dyson, a former NASA flight controller and National Geographic Explorer-in-Residence, Emeritus, for her invaluable expertise.

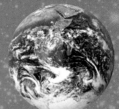

The pictures of the planets and other space objects in this book do not necessarily depict their sizes in proportion to each other. Exceptions appear on pages 8-9 and page 23, where the images are used to illustrate size relationships. In addition, some of the images of Neptune—the best images available from NASA at this time—show the Great Dark Spot, a storm that no longer exists.

Design by YAY! Design

Trade Paperback ISBN: 978-1-4263-1036-2

Reinforced library edition ISBN: 978-1-4263-1037-9

Photo Credits

cover, David Aguilar; 1, Earth Imaging/Getty Images; 2, NASA; 4-5, Tony Hallas/Science Faction/Corbis; 6-7, SuperStock; 8-9, NASA; 9 (top), NASA 10-11, NASA/Photo Researchers/Getty Images; 12 (left), Albert Klein/Oxford Scientific RM/Getty Images; 12 (right), Albert Klein/Oxford Scientific RM/Getty Images; 13 (left), David Aguilar; 13 (right), NASA; 14-15, SuperStock; 15 (left), Mikhail Markovskiy/Shutterstock; 15 (top right), Willyam Bradberry/Shutterstock; 15 (bottom right), Galyna Andrushko/Shutterstock; 16, NASA; 17, Steve A. Munsinger/Photo Researchers RM/Getty Images; 18 (bottom left), David Aguilar; 18 (bottom right), David Aguilar; 18 (center), David Aguilar; 18 (top), David Aguilar; 19, David Aguilar; 20 (top), Ian McKinnell/Getty Images; 20 (center), Albert Klein/Oxford Scientific RM/Getty Images; 20 (bottom), Albert Klein/Oxford Scientific RM/Getty Images; 21 (center), NASA; 21 (bottom), Dr. Mark Garlick; 22, Digital Vision/Getty Images; 23 (center), Albert Klein/Oxford Scientific RM/Getty Images; 23 (top), NASA; 23 (center), Albert Klein/Oxford Scientific RM/ Getty Images; 23 (bottom), NASA; 25, NASA/Science Source/Photo Researchers RM/ Getty Images; 26, Reuters/Corbis; 27, NASA/JPL-Caltech; 28, PhotoResearchers/Getty Images; 29, Ludek Pesek/National Geographic Stock; 30 (top), NASA; 30 (center), NASA; 30 (bottom), Photolink/Getty Images; 31 (top left), Ismael Jorda/Shutterstock; 31 (top right), NASA; 31 (bottom left), Image Source/Getty Images; 31 (bottom right), NASA; 32 (top left), David Aguilar; 32 (top right), Photolink/Photodisc/Getty Images; 32 (center left), NASA/ Photo Researchers RM/Getty Images; 32 (center right), NASA; 32 (bottom left), NASA; 32 (bottom right), Martin Fischer/Shutterstock; background, David Aguilar; header, David Aguilar; Space Clues, David Aguilar

National Geographic supports K—12 educators with ELA Common Core Resources.
Visit natgeoed.org/commoncore for more information.

Printed in the United States of America
15/WOR/3

Table of Contents

What's a Planet?

Circle, circle in the sky,
you're bright enough
to catch my eye.
You're not a star,
but a place
where gas or rocks
swirl in space.

Space Clues

GAS: Something that has no shape or size of its own. Gas can spread out into the space around it.

STAR: A huge ball of hot gas that makes heat and light

Hello, Planets!

When you look up high in the night sky, you might see lots of bright lights. Most of these lights are stars.

Space Clues

ORBIT: The path an object follows around another object, such as a star

REFLECT: To bounce back

Q What did two stars say to each other on Valentine's Day?

A I glow for you!

Most stars have planets moving around them. Planets are round objects that orbit a star. They don't create their own light. They only reflect light from stars.

The Sun

The sun is our star. Our planet Earth orbits the sun. The sun makes a lot of heat and light.

The sun

Don't look directly at the sun. It could hurt your eyes.

Its surface is about 100 times hotter than a hot summer day! It's also very big. One million Earths could fit inside the sun!

Earth

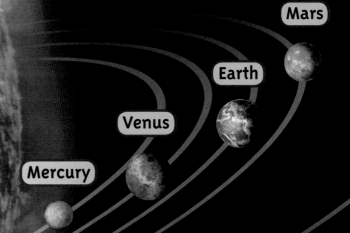

Mars

Earth

Venus

Mercury

Our sun and Earth are part of what we call our solar system. There are eight big planets and five small, dwarf planets in the solar system.

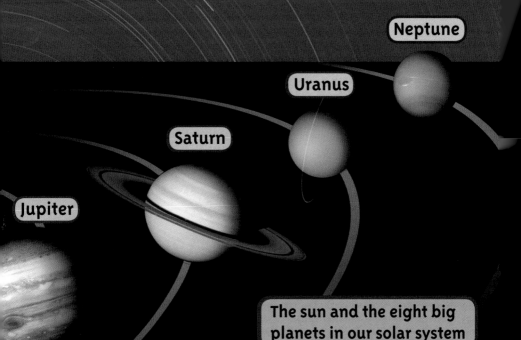

Neptune

Uranus

Saturn

Jupiter

The sun and the eight big planets in our solar system

Each planet orbits the sun. The strong pull of the sun's gravity holds the planets in orbit, which keeps them from floating away. Gravity is the same force that makes a baseball fall to the ground when you drop it.

Space Clues

GRAVITY: An invisible force that pulls objects toward a planet or star

The Inner Planets

Mercury, Venus, Earth, and Mars are in the hotter part of our solar system.

Venus

Mercury

Mars

Earth

These planets are the four closest
to the sun. They are made of rock
and metal.

Your Planet Earth

Earth is the third planet from the sun. The planet we call home spins at just the right distance from the sun.

It's far enough away to be not too hot, yet close enough so it's not too cold. Here, the conditions are just right for life.

sea animals

plants and trees

land animals

The Gas Giants

Saturn

rings

The gas giants do not have a hard surface like the rocky inner planets.

Jupiter

Neptune

Uranus

Saturn

Beyond the rocky inner planets, there are four gas giants. They are Jupiter, Saturn, Uranus (YOOR-eh-nes), and Neptune. These huge planets are made of big clouds of gas and liquid. Gravity pulls the gas and liquid into a planet shape.

All gas giants have rings. The rings are made of mostly ice and dust.

Dwarf Planets

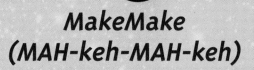

Dwarf planets are planetlike objects that are part of our solar system. They are much smaller than regular planets.

MakeMake (MAH-keh-MAH-keh)

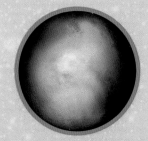

Ceres (SEER-eez)

Eris (EHR-is)

Pluto

This dwarf planet is shaped like an egg.

Haumea
(Ha-oo-MAY-ah)

A dwarf planet can be round or egg-shaped. Unlike regular planets, dwarf planets may share their orbits with other space objects.

Amazing Planets

These planets are really out of this world!

WEIRDEST SPIN

Uranus
This planet spins on its side, rolling like a barrel instead of a top.

WINDIEST WEATHER

Neptune
Winds on Neptune blow much faster than Earth's strongest hurricanes.

LONGEST-LASTING STORM

Jupiter

Great Red Spot

The Great Red Spot is a hurricane on Jupiter. It has been blowing for more than 400 years.

Venus

This is the solar system's hottest planet even though it is not the closest to the sun. A thick layer of gas around Venus makes it super hot.

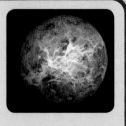

TALLEST MOUNTAIN

Mars

Mars is the home of the solar system's largest volcano, called Olympus Mons. It's as tall as three Mount Everests stacked up.

Olympus Mons

Mount Everest

Moons Galore!

Some planets, like Earth, have moons that travel with them. Moons are objects made of ice or rock that orbit a planet.

Some planets have no moons. Some have many. Jupiter has more than 60!

Jupiter and four of its moons

Jupiter

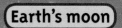
Earth's moon

Saturn has a giant moon called Titan. It is one of the largest moons in the solar system. It is even bigger than the planet Mercury!

Mercury

Titan

Our Moon

Earth has only one moon. It appears large and bright in the night sky.

Astronauts first walked on the moon more than 40 years ago. They left footprints in the dirt. There is no weather on the moon to wash or blow them away. Those footprints are still there.

Space Clues

WEATHER: The changing conditions that can include temperature, rainfall, wind, and clouds

Astronaut Buzz Aldrin walks on the moon in 1969 as part of the Apollo 11 mission.

Exploring Space

Scientists have many ways of studying planets. One is to visit them. Humans can't visit other planets yet. But we can send robots to explore them for us.

A rocket blasts off from Cape Canaveral, Florida. It is heading to Mars.

Robots called rovers have been sent to Mars. The rovers carry cameras and tools. They can take photographs and videos, too. The rovers send information back to Earth about what they see.

A drawing of a rover on Mars

telescope

There are other ways to learn about planets, too. Powerful telescopes allow us to see planets and moons even though they are far away.

270

Space probes also
collect information
about planets. These
spacecraft take pictures.
They measure light and
temperature, too.

With these tools, scientists make
exciting discoveries about other
worlds. What will we learn next?

Stump Your Parents

Can your parents answer these questions about planets? You might know more than they do!

Answers at bottom of page 31.

1

Which is NOT true about the sun?

A. It makes heat and light.
B. It is our planet's star.
C. It is much smaller than Earth.
D. Planets orbit around it.

2

What does Neptune have that's so special?

A. The largest volcano
B. The hottest surface
C. The weirdest spin
D. The windiest weather

3

What is Jupiter's Great Red Spot?

A. A moon
B. A volcano
C. A flood
D. A hurricane

4

Which planet has just one moon?
A. Mercury
B. Earth
C. Mars
D. Uranus

5

Which of these are the main materials found in planets' rings?
A. Gas
B. Ice
C. Dust
D. B and C

6

What can you use to get a better view of objects in space?
A. Microscopes
B. Telescopes
C. Submarines
D. Flashlights

7

To study the environment on Mars, scientists have sent ____.
A. Rovers
B. Airplanes
C. Space shuttles
D. Astronauts

Planet Earth

GAS: Something that has no shape or size of its own. Gas can spread out into the space around it.

GRAVITY: An invisible force that pulls objects toward a planet or star

ORBIT: The path an object follows around another object, such as a star

REFLECT: To bounce back

STAR: A huge ball of hot gas that makes heat and light

WEATHER: The changing conditions that can include temperature, rainfall, wind, and clouds